"In *Touch the Earth*, Drew Jackson's poetry offers a word-weary world a new language of engagement, disruption, and insight. As with all great poetry, the words are spare, but the literary i̶m̶a̶g̶e̶s̶ ... impressions on the reader. Like echo  sound, the poems stay with you, they the poem 'Shake the Dust,' I am still c of *power*, one no longer confined to pressors but with a conscience as stic its memories to be shaken loose. This collection is a meditative treasure."

Barbara Holmes, author of *Joy Unspeakable: Contemplative Practices of the Black Church* and *Crisis Contemplation: Healing the Wounded Village*

"*Touch the Earth* is an interdisciplinary work full of Blackness, divinity, grief, community, and many other elements of life that make us human, specific yet universal. It's not a text that one can digest quickly. Each word has to seep into the grooves of the body."

Morgan Jerkins, senior editor of ZORA magazine and author of *This Will Be My Undoing*

"I'm one of those people who likes the idea of reading poetry more than actually reading it. Occasionally, however, I stumble on a poet like Drew Jackson, whose lyrical language and urgent themes set a hook in me. Drawing on the liberating Jesus of Luke's Gospel, Jackson explores heritage, history, and a longing for freedom. *Touch the Earth* pushes back against the spirit of scarcity and invites readers into an achingly authentic spirituality. Whether you are a 'poetry person' or not, this book will leave you mesmerized."

Jonathan Merritt, contributing writer for the *Atlantic* and author of *Learning to Speak God from Scratch*

"Drew Jackson's poetry touches something very deep in me as he exposes truths not easily spoken of directly and yet truths that must be told . . . and faced. I pray you will partake of Drew's newest collection of poems with an open heart and an open Bible, engaging familiar stories with new and different eyes. Promise me you will not rush through them but that you will sit still and ponder, for a very long time, on what these things might mean. Promise me you will sit with the questions these poems raise until God speaks and tells you what is yours to do in response. I know that's what I will be doing!"

Ruth Haley Barton, founder of the Transforming Center and author of *Strengthening the Soul of Your Leadership*

"This collection is a companion for mystics and storytellers alike. Poem after poem, Drew Jackson approaches questions of community and trust and meets them not with the bore of certainty but a reverence for the unspoken, for mystery and suspense. Jackson's words will leave you waiting in the silence . . . but never alone."

Cole Arthur Riley, creator of Black Liturgies and author of *This Here Flesh*

"There are seasons for prose and seasons for poetry, and we find ourselves, certainly, in the latter. I can think of no better guide and no more insightful voice for this moment than Drew Jackson's. Drew's ability to challenge and surprise through language and rhythm is unparalleled, and I'm so grateful for these poems."

Shauna Niequist, author of *I Guess I Haven't Learned That Yet* and *Present Over Perfect*

"In *Touch the Earth*, Drew Jackson gives us language for how to move through the earth and toward one another."

Ekemini Uwan, public theologian and cohost of *Truth's Table Podcast*

Foreword by
Pádraig
Ó Tuama

TOUCH
THE
EARTH

Poems on The Way

Drew Jackson

An imprint of InterVarsity Press
Downers Grove, Illinois

InterVarsity Press
P.O. Box 1400 | Downers Grove, IL 60515-1426
ivpress.com | email@ivpress.com

InterVarsity Press® is the publishing division of InterVarsity Christian Fellowship/USA®. For more information, visit intervarsity.org.

While any stories in this book are true, some names and identifying information may have been changed to protect the privacy of individuals.

Quote in the poem "Streets Is Talking" is from Jay-Z, "Streets Is Talking," *The Dynasty: Roc La Familia*, Roc-A-Fella/Def Jam, 2000.

Quote in the poem "A Harvest of Dreamers" is from Langston Hughes, *The Collected Poems of Langston Hughes* (New York: Alfred A. Knopf/Vintage, 1994).

Quote in the poem "Pray Then Like This" is from Martin Luther King Jr., "King Quotes on War and Peace," The Martin Luther King, Jr. Research and Education Institute, Stanford University, https://kinginstitute .stanford.edu/liberation-curriculum/classroom-resources/king-quotes-war-and-peace, accessed March 23, 2022.

Quote in the poem "Kiss of Death" is from Leon Huff, Gene McFadden, John Whitehead, "Back Stabbers," The O'Jays, *Back Stabbers*, Philadelphia International, 1972.

The publisher cannot verify the accuracy or functionality of website URLs used in this book beyond the date of publication.

Cover design and image composite: David Fassett
Interior design: Daniel van Loon

ISBN 978-1-5140-0269-8 (print) | ISBN 978-1-5140-0270-4 (digital)

Printed in the United States of America ∞

Library of Congress Cataloging-in-Publication Data
Names: Jackson, Drew E., 1989- author.
Title: Touch the earth : poems on the way / Drew Jackson.
Other titles: Touch the earth (Compilation)
Description: Downers Grove, IL : InterVarsity Press, [2022]
Identifiers: LCCN 2022035646 (print) | LCCN 2022035647 (ebook) | ISBN
   9781514002698 (paperback) | ISBN 9781514002704 (ebook)
Subjects: LCSH: Bible. Luke, IX-XXIV—Poetry. | Christian poetry, American.
   | LCGFT: Religious poetry.
Classification: LCC PS3610.A3494 T68 2022 (print) | LCC PS3610.A3494
   (ebook) | DDC 811/.6—dc23/eng/20220808
LC record available at https://lccn.loc.gov/2022035646
LC ebook record available at https://lccn.loc.gov/2022035647

30 29 28 27 26 25 24 23 | 13 12 11 10 9 8 7 6 5 4 3 2 1

For Pop

The man who taught me that faith is more than talk.

The glory of God is a human being fully alive.

St. Irenaeus

CONTENTS

PART II: JERUSALEM

Foreword

Pádraig Ó Tuama

What is a gospel? Nobody knows really.

Of course, we kind of do: there are four gospels—a word meaning *good news*—accepted as part of the Christian Scriptures. And there are other gospels too: the Gospel of Thomas, the Gospel of Mary Magdalene. Whether accepted as canonical or not, whether written thirty or three hundred years after the execution of Jesus of Nazareth, there is a broad consensus that gospel is a form of literature.

The word is heard elsewhere too. "What kind of music are you into?" someone might ask. *Gospel*, someone would respond, and everybody with good taste nods their head in respect.

"Is that the truth?" someone might ask. *Gospel*, someone might reply.

But still, the question is, What is a gospel? Was it a brand-new form of literature invented two thousand years ago? In a way, that's kind of true. Gospel is at once a biography of a character—most often Jesus, son of Mary—but also a presentation of their political, theological, and social ideology. Do the gospels all agree? On some things, yes, but each gospel emerged in its own context, borrowing here, modifying there. What is gospel? It's hard to know exactly, but what we do know is that it's a genre less concerned with chronology than it is with community: how to act in the face of an empire; how to notice small moments of life; how to be interrupted; how to assert dignity in the face of demeaning treatment; how to challenge rules for a greater good; how to create common cause; how to get through.

So we have a genre, and here, in *Touch the Earth*, we have a response to a genre.

Drew Jackson has at least three areas of deep study: the gospels, poetry, and community. He reads the gospels through the lens of the other two. He loves poetry—I've seen his glorious bookshelves, and we've spoken about the books on those shelves. He also studies community. Sitting in his church one Sunday listening to him speak about Rev. Dr. Martin Luther King's vision of the Beloved Community, I was struck by how community, poetry, and gospel are one thing for Drew. In *Touch the Earth* he uses his precise words to open up worlds of inquiry: How to read a text about redemption during an era of police violence? How to honor Black life? How to live in the wake of grief? How to love language while words are being cheapened in public life? How to hold images of war alongside images of giggling children you pick up after school? What do you do with the memory of the shoeless man you passed on the way to church?

These poems are a wrestle. They do not offer answers. I know that Drew believes in God, but I'm unsure if he believes in answers—they are too easy, and Drew is more likely to discomfit than he is to decorate.

Through craft and question, through elegy (his mother sings in these poems) and imagination, through curiosity and compassion, Drew has written a poetic response to the Gospels—the second in a series, the first being *God Speaks Through Wombs*—that shows what happens when you take language seriously: the language offered by religious literature; the language of public life; the language of private consideration; the language of community action. We go from the walkways of Jerusalem to those of Manhattan; we hear words of a mother and wonder whether it's the mother of Jesus or Drew (*yes*, is the answer); we hear empire's demands and then hear Drew's prayers for empire's doom. *Touch the Earth* is built on study: of literature, of life, of poetry, of friendship, of love. *Touch the Earth* is built on a theological imagination that takes the body seriously. *Touch the Earth* is built on a life of practice and love. It is a treasure of linguistic skill. It is also an invitation.

PART I

JOURNEY

I

STUDENTS

Touch the Earth

Luke 9:1-2

My father says more with his hands than he does with his lips. I cannot
recall him
    sitting me down

to teach me about love, but I watched him tend to my mother
    as cancer spread through her insides.

He cried when her breath left her, though he never lectured me about grief.

I am still grieving my mother,
still
gleaning what my father taught me.

Gather it from memory.
Let it touch the earth.

Take Nothing

Luke 9:3-4

I have nothing to take anyway.
Life has been a game of learning to navigate

this world without much in my bag.
I was taught to brag about our resourcefulness.

The way the coarse hands of our mothers stitch together
clothing and stories out of what was garbage

is the stuff of gods. All things new.
Our mantra—*poor in possessions but rich in family.*

Common understanding: *we all we got.*
Warm up a pot. Pull up a chair.

SHAKE THE DUST

Luke 9:5-6

It is never easy to forget.
The conscience is not so forgiving.
It must be made of cling wrap—
getting stuck to anything
it contacts.

I learned a trick:
store it in the freezer
to reduce its clinginess.
But isn't that its power?
The way it can't shake anything?
The way everything sticks?

In Their Garden

Luke 9:7-9

You can kill a revolutionary,
but you can never kill the revolution.
FRED HAMPTON

And the truth is
they can never
put us down.

Like weeds in their garden.

Pull us out
and we will
pop up again.

Dead dandelion.
Seedhead floating through the air.
Falling to the ground.

House of Hunting, House of the Hunter

Luke 9:10

The soul is like a wild animal–tough, resilient, savvy,
self-sufficient and yet exceedingly shy.
Parker J. Palmer, *A Hidden Wholeness*

I run here when I am hunted.
        Camouflage amongst the cedars.
Keep quiet with the doe.
        Hold my breath. Wipe my sweat
Before it hits the leaves below.

On the hunt, I run here.
        First crash, then tiptoe.
Wait for its emergence.
        Spot its shape in the shadows.
Afraid of what might lurk there.

SILENCE DISRUPTED

Luke 9:11

Pop worked long hours,
so the weekend was a haven for him—

the length of Saturday spent in the cave
of his bedroom.

Tiger Woods hitting drives down the center of the green
on the TV screen.

A bag of Hot Cheese Curls
already half-eaten.

I could hear him drifting in and out of sleep,
as snores vibrated the hallway walls.

The voice that we all have
whispered on the inside:

He'd rather not be bothered

But like the shot heard 'round the world
I would burst through the doorway,

plopping my body next to his
lying sideways across the bed.

That's when he said
How's it going, bud?

And I knew I was welcome
to settle in.

We Feed Each Other

Luke 9:12-17

"It's still that black abundance?" I asked LaThon.
"You already know."
KIESE LAYMON, *HEAVY*

There isn't enough to go around—
the engine that drives our way of life.

We've been sold this narrative, and bought it
at the open-air market of neoclassical economics.

Scarcity.
The limited availability of a commodity.

Five loaves and two fish
will only get you so far.

But we were taught *ujamaa*
before we internalized the empire's mantra.

Blessing and breaking
what little we have.

LEFTOVERS

Luke 9:17

Never show up to the cookout
or slide through the fish fry
without some Tupperware in hand.
You won't want to miss
the blessing of these leftovers
for days on end.
The best hosts always provide
take home containers.
Take as much as you want, child.
There's plenty to go around.

STREETS IS TALKING

Luke 9:18-21

After Jay-Z's "Streets Is Talking"

Know this:
people will talk.

    They will form opinions
    and rehearse them to strangers
    as known fact.

I sat in the back of my brother's Mazda 929.
The *Dynasty* album flooding my ten-year-old ears.
Jay-Z's inquisitive lyrics:

    Is he a Blood, is he Crip?
    Is he that, is he this?

I listened to find out
for myself.

CRAZY TALK

Luke 9:22

I.
What I say only sounds crazy
to those who have paid no attention.
The powers that be
are as predictable as the seasons.
With them it is no secret:
when they have pegged you as a threat
you might as well have signed your death warrant.

II.
What I say only sounds crazy
to those who have paid no attention.
Their party or position is of little account:
    challenge their power,
    ruffle their feathers,
    rouse the people to dream for better,
they will collude to take you out.

III.
What I say only sounds crazy
to those who have paid no attention.
Watch the seasons—how winter changes to spring.
Has death ever truly been an end?
Resurrection sounds far-fetched
until you observe the crocus each year,
and the fact that we, as a people, are even still here.

Sōtēr, Pt. II

Luke 9:23-27

To write a history of passing is to write a history of loss.
Allyson Hobbs, Stanford historian

I do not know who I am.
I have been told who I am.

By the sarcastic *good luck* of brothers
when I share my dreams.

By the smothering love of mothers
that would not let me leave.

By the silence of my father
who I wished would speak.

By oppressive words and laws
that would not let me free.

These have taught me how I must be.
Internalized in my psyche, deep.

This mask I wear so no one knows,
I gain the world but lose my soul.

Like Dunbar said *we wear the mask.*
It grins and lies and lets me pass.

But passing is a false salvation.
This daily death, my liberation.

INNER CIRCLE

Luke 9:28

She is a friend of my mind. She gather me, man. The pieces I am, she
gather them and give them back to me in all the right order.
TONI MORRISON, *BELOVED*

I once took a personality test that said I was a magnet—
                                        an attractor of people.
        I have a strong pull.

I can pull together
                                        parts of me
        in any order.

Smile from my father. Wit from my mother.
                                I know what to cover
        to be liked.

Loved in the presence of two since grade school days.
                                        They made room
        for all of me.

The room of me. The part of me that I parted with
                                        in the company
        of others.

TRANSFIGURED

Luke 9:28-36

*There is no way of telling people that they are all walking around shining
like the sun. . . . If only they could all see themselves as they really are.*
THOMAS MERTON, CONJECTURES OF A GUILTY BYSTANDER

I have known mountains.

My place of prayer,
where the air is not thick
with shame.
There, Mom visits—
offering prophetic words
like she did when she was more
than just a memory, saying:

Abide.
Everything else
will take care of itself.

Down in the valley
the shadow of death broods.
Badges. Batons that bruise.
Voices repeating:

Whose car is this?
I can smell
the alcohol
all over you.

I climb.
Every chance.
I get.

Reminded.
I shine.
Like the sun.

THE TRAGEDY OF
THE DISINHERITED

Luke 9:37-43

The doom of the children is the greatest tragedy of the disinherited.
HOWARD THURMAN, JESUS AND THE DISINHERITED

Down in the valley,
in the belly of this beast,
Tamir can't run free.
The Emmetts are threatened

till their young bodies are
seized by the demonic,
squeezed out of the life
that others enjoy.

And we are left helpless
in the face of the evil
that is suffocating
our sons.

Wondering what else can be done,
we begin to lose faith
that any change
can come.

So we *lift our eyes to the hills,*
questioning
when and where
our help will come from.

HUMAN HANDS

Luke 9:43-45

The hands that run Guantánamo.
The hands that build concentration camps
and handle bodies as profane commodities.

The hands that ball themselves into fists to strike.
The hands that contort themselves to draft abusive laws
and grip the profit that comes as a result.

The hands that hold doors for dictators and despots.
The hands that roll out red carpets for tyrants
and raise themselves in agreement with evil.

The hands that reach and grab without consent.
The hands that lay themselves on Bibles
and swear that she did not say no.

The hands that are attached to itchy trigger fingers.
The hands that turn off body cameras
and scrub the blood that is on them.

The hands that hold pieces of silver after a kiss of betrayal.
The hands that slap cuffs on innocent wrists
and twist to make it slightly more painful.

The hands that burn Omaha down.
The hands that castrate and lynch Will Brown
and then write history books with no such memory.

The hands that wash themselves of all responsibility.
The hands that wear neutrality's promise ring
and never lift a finger to help those being crushed.

And What of Greatness?

Luke 9:46-48

You might think it strange to hear boys from the hood with constant talk of goats on our lips. Does. Nannies. Bucks. Billies. But my boys and I want to be like Ali. *Floating like butterflies and stinging like bees.* Punching our way to the top of the totem. Can you blame us? We just want to rise above what's expected of us.

And what of greatness?

To reach the standard the empire's portrayed,
we must learn how to play the empire's game.

WITH OR AGAINST

Luke 9:49-50

Declaration:
he is my enemy.

He does not exorcise
the way I prefer.

He refers to demons
as unclean spirits.

In my estimation,
he does not correctly name
the issue.

Never mind that we both
want the evil cast out.
I have concerns with
the way he goes about it.

Him against me.
And the evil
goes free.

LIKE FLINT

Luke 9:51-53

There is nothing like my dog when he is on a mission:
sniffing, his nostrils twitching up and down
nose nearly touching the ground
tracking the scent of some delight
that he's determined to find.

His eyes, normally wide, squint
like almonds.
His lips curl upward, exposing teeth,
at any attempt to redirect.

If only I could be so intent—
my scent set on delight,
resolved to revel
in the goodness of the world,
but I fear such a single-minded life.

A Rebuke

Luke 9:54-56

It is easy to call down fire,
much harder to rain down mercy.

The Call in Three Movements

Luke 9:57-62

I spoke foolishly in my youth,
often not considering consequences.
I would go without knowing
where I might arrive or
whether those on the receiving end
might welcome me inside.
I just wanted to be free.
He made me consider the price tag.

• • •

When you are raised under the weight
of a regime that cares nothing for
your well-being, you have to look out
for your own.
I was taught to always show honor
in a land that dishonors us.
So when I ponder his call to follow
I know that family must come first.

• • •

My father once left our home
for a routine trip to the store
and never returned. After that
it became common practice
to always say our goodbyes.
Go on ahead
I'll catch up with you in due time.

II

Neighbors

Squad Up

Luke 10:1

Like that time after school
    when all my boys came out of the woodwork.

You didn't expect us to roll so deep
    when you said *meet me in the park.*

Did you think there were only
    a few of us? My crew runs about 70 to 72.

A Harvest of Dreamers

Luke 10:2

After Langston Hughes's "Dreams"

There is a direct connection
between our capacity to imagine
and our ability to see.

> *We were like those who dream*
> until they stole our fortunes
> and trampled on our ambition.

We are born with a proclivity
to visualize beyond the visible.
We honed this skill as children.

> They pilfered our progeny,
> robbed our hope of a future harvest,
> and turned our artists into puppets.

Hold fast to dreams.
The farmer sees
the yield before the field produces.

> Our wings have been clipped.
> This field
> *frozen with snow.*

ROMULUS AND REMUS

Luke 10:3

I have been called a *superpredator*—
less than a human being, ready
to commit violent crimes without remorse.
Perceived as some mythological creature
to be captured and chained,
forever to remain behind bars.
This way of thinking has seized
hearts and minds like a pathogen,
under the guise of being tough on crime.

I am no predator, I am prey—
my body locked within the gaze
of those who have been raised
by wolves. I cannot conceive
of the day when we will lie down together.

Instructions for the Freedom Struggle

Luke 10:4-12

I.   Empty out the money bag.
      Freedom cannot be bought, but it can

      be sold
      away.

      Inscribe this line on your insides:
      Relationships are the currency of life.

II.   Attire yourself with nothing
      but the finery of dust.

      The less you have
      the harder it is to be

      weighed down.

III. Bolt the goal in view.
      Let nothing unfasten
      your vision
      from what's ahead.

IV. Drink to the dregs
      every ounce of hospitality.

      Scrape each crumb from the plate of love
      set before you.

V. Know when to bless.
Know when to dissent.

There is an art to protest.
Draw your lines

with precision.

Maledictions

Luke 10:13-16

I grew up in a *watch your mouth* kind of house. Our tongues were met with black peppercorn, cayenne, and Louisiana Red if we were flippant with the things we said. Threats of mouths washed out with soap were not unheard of. Mom stayed ready, armed with a bar of Dove.

Curses were lazy talk. Speech filler. An indication that we needed to stretch our lexicon.

Perhaps we needed to bury our heads in another book. The good one, in which I read:

There is a time for everything.

Which I interpreted to mean there must be a time for pronouncing damnation. Damned be this nation that rejects the miracle of our humanity. Cursed be this city that remains silent while our bodies are crucified and swinging from trees.

POWER TO THE PEOPLE

Luke 10:17-19

The most common way people give up their power
is by thinking they don't have any.
ALICE WALKER

This is a tactic
used by men who sit in Caesar's seat:
convince the people they are weak,
impotent and wholly reliant
on those in high places.

But since creation's dawn
God has maintained
what Bobby Seale and Huey Newton
made famous:

Power to the people.

This is the work:
to realize what is already ours
and not to be surprised
when the demons tremble.

To Live and
to Live On

Luke 10:20

I would give anything to be met
with the rush again:
success in this crowded room,
packed with failure.

A fleeting Eden.

Apokalypsis
(Tell Me)

Luke 10:21-24

Tell me how to see.

Tell me why all who have eyes
do not detect light.
And what is the corrective
to this condition?

Tell me about vision,
by which I mean intuition,
insight, and the ability to see inside
the complexities of life.

Tell me why the children can dream,
and have no trouble seeing another world,
while we, with all manner of worldly wisdom,
remain conception impaired.

Tell me about despair.

Touch Yo' Neighbor

Luke 10:25-29

I heard the pastor say,
Go on and touch yo' neighbor.

After I watched her fold a mucus-filled tissue
and tuck it back into her purse.

She must've never learned
to cough into her chicken wing.

I can't believe she just reached
for a communion cracker.

I think I'll pass today.

Nobody Talks About the Road

Luke 10:30-37

It is not enough to aid the wounded man on the Jericho Road. It is also necessary to work to change the conditions of the Jericho Road which made robbery possible.
MARTIN LUTHER KING JR.

Nobody talks about the road,
save for Martin
and every prophet under heaven's sky.

To me it is no surprise
why we focus
on a compassionate act.

Does it not cause your brow to furrow
that this thoroughfare
is known for its bloodlust?

Adummim.

Nobody talks about the road.

For Those Who Choose to Sit

Luke 10:38-42

Arrest me for sitting on a bus? You may do that.

Rosa Parks

There's something about sitting where you have been told not to sit.
At the front of a bus. At a counter for lunch. Right up at the feet of Jesus.

My mother walked into our independent, fundamental Baptist church
and sat on the pew wearing a pair of blue Levi's.

She was invited to help the school students with their theater projects,
but it was assumed she'd wear a full-length skirt.

She was scolded, told to change, then to come back.
That's okay, she said, then packed her bag and drove home.

Every single student she was set to work with followed and they
rehearsed in our living room, learning techniques, sitting at her feet.

III

PRAYER

A Certain Place

Luke 11:1

Could be any place.
Any space where the veil
between heaven and earth is thin.

Observing the drips
from the street above
while the L train runs behind schedule.

Walking Baxter,
as he sniffs for the right spot
to do what creatures do.

Kneeling at the altar
of my daughter's bedside,
wiping the tears caused by a bad dream.

Listening to each keystroke
as this poem
takes shape on a screen.

CURIOUS OBSERVATION

Luke 11:1

sometimes i wonder how they watch me
as i sit in this chair each day,
this
fixed spot in front of my windowsill
silent and still,
like i watched my mother
as she sat on the back patio
and wondered
what was happening inside
her silent world.
i wonder if one day they will ask,
like i asked,
about what happens there
in that chair
or will they not care at all.

Pray Then Like This

Luke 11:2-4

Our.

Yours and mine.
It ties us. Binds us together—

an inescapable network of mutuality,
a single garment of destiny.

We share an end, a beginning.
Only one us
in this thing we call living.

It is fitting that we start here.
Maybe we should stop here.

Imagine, or, Suppose

Luke 11:5-8

The line between
imagination and prayer
is as thin as air.

Thoughts on Asking, Seeking, and Knocking

Luke 11:9-10

One of my elders, I can't remember which, told me
to never let anything keep me from asking.
The worst you can be told is no.

I have wondered about rejection,
whether it is a reflection of my skill
or, at times, my skin.

As kids we played knock knock zoom zoom,
or ding dong ditch, depending on which
region of the country you came up in.

There were certain doors we wouldn't knock on.
We were afraid that maybe
they would open.

ODE TO POP

Luke 11:11-13

My dad let my friends call him Pop,
which is what we called him too.
Generous is the word I would use to describe him,
for he would give and give and give
until his insides burst open with compassion.
His endless flow of bestowing on us what we need,
and sometimes what we want, never stops.
Some would say this is his fatal flaw,
by which I mean
he would gladly go to his grave empty-handed.
This is the man who gave up valuable work hours
to shower me with encouragement and praise
after every little league and high school game.
The same man who sold his car dealership
because those Dodge minivans were stealing
precious minutes from his children.

Silenced

Luke 11:14

There's really no such thing as the "voiceless." There are only
the deliberately silenced, or the preferably unheard.
Arundhati Roy

There is a difference between silence
and being silenced.
Only one of these involves
the violence of demons.

These henchmen of hell
force their hands on our mouths,
those with so-called power, afraid
of what we might conjure.

THIS HAUNTED HOUSE

Luke 11:15-26

If I could save the Union without freeing any slave I would do it,
and if I could save it by freeing all slaves I would do it.
ABRAHAM LINCOLN

Lincoln spoke of a house divided.
He did not want this house to fall.
It will become all one thing or all the other.
Which *all* it became was not Mr. Lincoln's concern.

To preserve is to maintain something in its existing state,
no matter if that state is slave.
They will go to their graves for the Union,
not for all to be recognized, under the law, as human.

But this man who spoke four score
and many more years before Lincoln
was not interested
in preserving the union of a haunted house.

Cast them out
and let it fall!

REDEMPTION

Luke 11:21-26

Redemption, the rollback to Reconstruction, unfolded on two planes—
one was political, and that was disenfranchising black men who had
been allowed to vote because of the Reconstruction Acts . . . and then
secondly, instituting a system of peonage and sharecropping, which
is as close to slavery as you can get without actually being slavery.
HENRY LOUIS GATES JR.

On June 19, 1865
they cast out a demon
named Chattel.

For a few years it wandered,
looking
for a place to lay its head.

It returned to find
a reconstructed house
with plenty of space for friends.

Their names were:
Jim and Jane
KKK
Lynching
Sharecropping
Convict leasing
Voter suppression

These friends
became residents and
made themselves at home.

And the last state
of the person
is worse than the first.

BLESSEDNESS

Luke 11:27-28

Dear Mama . . . you are appreciated.
TUPAC SHAKUR

This is not a poem about a mother's work,
or about a woman's worth
being tied to her work as a mother.

Your raising of us four—
the way your organs were displaced
to make space as you bore us,

how you sat up late nights, *with Jesus
on the mainline,* sharing
all your wants.

Rising with the sun to wake us,
making sure we were together
before rushing to the bus stop.

This was only a portion.

You worked words with your pen.
Became a pundit of the paint palette
in your basement studio.

Frustrater of tyrants—
you insisted on you,
refusing to be diminished.

Then there was the gift.
Your atmosphere—
the air of belonging.

This is not a poem about a mother's work,
or about a woman's worth
being tied to her work as a mother.

The Sign of Jonah

Luke 11:29-36

In my generation
many have forsaken
the four walls.

We prefer church in the wild,
providing sanctuary
from corrupt governments.

We raise our hallelujah on the protest line,
standing eye to eye
with police in riot gear.

We are partial to prayer meetings in the streets,
less movement of the mouth
more marching of the feet.

No other sign will be given.
The revolution will not be televised.

WASHING DISHES

Luke 11:37-41

As a kid I washed dishes—
Mom always insisted on a deep clean.
Swift wipe downs of outside surfaces
were insufficient.
Sponges and dish rags squeezing their way
into every crack and crevice.
Leaving no evidence of yesterday's
red Kool-Aid, left out for a day, now sticky,
clinging to the bottom edges of the cup,
better not show up when Mom
goes to offer our guest a beverage.

WEIGHTIER MATTERS

Luke 11:42-44

meaning heavy,
as if to say my back
arms and legs
do not have the strength
to carry more—
the poundage too much
to shoulder alone

• • •

meaning important,
as though I should devote
what little time I have
on this planet
to nothing else—
no filling my schedule
with things of lesser consequence

• • •

meaning powerful,
as if to suggest
that the force of these
is sufficient to shake the world
and break open a stone-enclosed heart

WHEN THE TRUTH INSULTS ME

Luke 11:45

I ask myself, whose truth?
Or is there even one—singular,
some certitude etched in stone
by a divine finger, which then points
itself at me, detailing
every way that I have fallen short.

What I really mean to say is,
I've been exposed—cut open
by a double-edged word,
left red with my own insecurities,
now fragrant, for the sharks
to encircle and eat me alive.

Monuments

Luke 11:46-54

With this faith, we will be able to hew out of the
mountain of despair a stone of hope.
MARTIN LUTHER KING JR.

Out of a mountain of hope,
a stone of despair erected there
on government grounds
where the hounds of hell
once plotted assassination,
where mouths now tell tales
of a fabricated story—
heaping glory
on the dreamer once dubbed
the most dangerous man
in all the land.
We chisel monuments.
Blood drips
from our hands.

IV

HYPOCRISY

Meanwhile

Luke 12:1

They gathered
    by thousands
in steeple-topped
    buildings,
on pew's edge,
    waiting
for a word.

Amens
    so loud
they smothered
    the sound
of bones
    being crushed
underfoot.

Hypocrisy

Luke 12:1-3

Mom and Pop used to tell me,
don't try and hide things from us,
we'll find out.

This scared me.
I thought they would tear
apart my room

in search of
the slightest misstep,
or interrogate

every friend that
passed through the portals
of our home.

Now I know
they were simply
teaching me

about the
self-disclosing nature
of a lie.

Eyes on the Sparrow

Luke 12:4-7

Birds flying high, you know how I feel . . .
It's a new dawn, it's a new day, it's a new life for me.
And I'm feeling good.

NINA SIMONE, "FEELING GOOD"

I have known fear, calling it *failed expectations*. I have traversed the world of my soul in search of myself, only to find an apparition—the specter of who you expect me to be. I am no standard bearer, even though you have heaped this title on me. Your praise has become my idol, trembling at the thought of your wrath if I do not pass your test—if I do not achieve your measure of success. Do the sparrows live under the same stress as I do? Is their flight inhibited because of what others insist their lives should be? They glide so freely, catching their wings on the breeze of oblivion.

BLASPHEMY

Luke 12:8-12

There is a river.
It flows from glory to glory,
going wherever it wills.

Its streams spill
over their banks—
a deluge of grace,

soaking
the face of the earth
right through to its core,

becoming life
for those who stand
in the roar of its waters.

ODE TO THE SAVINGS ACCOUNT

Luke 12:13-21

I remember days when I knew nothing
of a savings account.
Our funds only enough
to get us to the next paycheck.
Praises were on deck
when that Chase push notification came through.
And I'm not saying that now I've made it,
but I can differentiate
between a 401(k) and a Roth IRA.
I've noticed
that the praises have lessened.
Rather, have been directed
elsewhere.

Pigeon Economics

Luke 12:22-34

*New York City is experiencing the highest rate of homelessness
since the Great Depression. For every 1 person experiencing
homelessness here, there are ~3 vacant apartments.*

Rep. Alexandria Ocasio-Cortez

I live in New York City
so I will consider the pigeons,
                    gathering
around Union Square benches,
                    sharing
french fries that have fallen
from the fingers of friends
on their lunch breaks,
                    knowing
that crumbs are abundant
in a place like this,
                    giving
laughter to children
in awe of their power
to make the birds scatter,
                    sheltering
from the coming rain
beneath the overhang
of the nearby Barnes & Noble,
                    living
free because
what they need
is never scarce.

FOUR BOYS

Luke 12:35-48

Summertime.
Mom would leave the house around 9am

every Friday
to bring the Spice back to the curls of her hair

after a week
of wear and tear.

Pop was at work
and so the house was left to be managed

by us four boys.
She hoped she'd return to find

nothing damaged.
But I said four boys. We knew nothing

of tending.
We were far more acquainted with

upending.

MILES

Luke 12:49-53

Don't play what's there. Play what's not there.
MILES DAVIS

Miles broke all the rules.
tradition
      be damned
when a new jam was brewing

He had
      no interest in reinventing
old tunes

ALWAYS new
always NEW
no need for another *Kind of Blue*

      many called it
         the end of jazz

It was TOO different
causing
      di/vi/si/on
within the genre

We tend to call
di
    vis
      ive
what we have
      no {category} for

When the Rain Comes

Luke 12:54-59

What do I do when the rain comes?
It's amazing,
we know when the rain
is coming.

> The rain is coming
> and I know not to wear
> my all-white Js
> because of what the rain will do.

Because of what the rain will do
I adjust how I proceed.
I do not leave the house
without an umbrella.

> We are the umbrella, shielding
> each other from the storm
> that is coming, huddled
> under a canopy of love.

Love, like a canopy, covers
a multitude of sins,
it ushers in
a new world.

> A new world is in bloom,
> its predictable movements
> only hidden from us
> who refuse to see—

hidden from us who refuse
to read the tea leaves
and adjust
how we proceed.

I will proceed with love
and find cover
in the secret place
when the rain comes.

V

TYRANTS

There Are Pontius
Pilates in Every Age

Luke 13:1

We have never preached violence, except the violence of love, which left
Christ nailed to a cross. . . . The violence we preach is not the violence of
the sword, the violence of hatred. It is the violence of love, of brotherhood,
the violence that wills to beat weapons into sickles for work.

St. Óscar Romero, *The Violence of Love*

When they killed Rutilio Grande, it changed the Archbishop. He understood then that if the government would kill a Jesuit priest to keep the poor in their place, he must take on the same commitment as his friend. From then on he was in it with the campesinos.

He once wrote a letter to Jimmy Carter, pleading that the US stop funding the slaughter of the Salvadoran people.

He even confronted Pope John Paul II, attempting to obtain a Vatican condemnation of the regime's violations of human rights. They never issued one, instead asking him to focus on unifying the priests. In other words, to keep quiet.

Quite to the dismay of popes and government agents, he chose to broadcast his message weekly, from the radio station. He filled each Sunday sermon with lists of those who were murdered. His words kept the people informed. More than that, kept them dreaming of something more.

On that day in 1980, March 24, he called on Salvadoran soldiers to stop obeying the government's abusive orders. Word must have gotten around, because as the sun went down and he finished the celebration of Mass, a red car drove past and put a bullet in his chest.

Shot dead while the crucified Jesus looked on.

SURVIVOR'S GUILT

Luke 13:2-9

I was in 7th grade,
Ms. Hunter's English class.

She stepped out of the room, only to bring back news
of the towers being struck. In that moment, we all were

hit with the kind of awe that leaves you speechless,
but also wondering—is there more to come?

I asked questions, although I was hesitant
to know the answers:

Who did this? And why did they choose to turn airplanes
into rockets, leaving their red glare across the sky?

How many died? Are there still some left crying
for help underneath the rubble?

Is this judgment of some sort, like the televangelists say?
Will I ever ride in an airplane again?

Did we bring this on ourselves—we, being America,
the land of the free that occupies the lands of others?

Why not me, since I was just in New York City
gazing up at those buildings three weeks prior?

Why us? As if American lives
should be exempt from terror.

To Become a Flower

Luke 13:10-11

I spend my time analyzing the dirt,
my eyes always in its direction.

It's been a long while since I've seen my reflection
in the eyes of another person.

I prefer the dirt. It doesn't look back at me
with its judgment.

I do not have to wonder if the dirt will welcome me,
it is where I am from and where I am going.

I would call it home, but that is not a comforting thought.
Home is where I learned I ought to look at people

when they speak to me. It is also where I fell in love
with the dust of the ground—

where I learned the world would be better off with me
not around.

I'd rather give my life to the dirt,
proving my worth by becoming fertilizer.

Maybe then I will become a flower,
with the courage to lift my face toward heaven.

WHICH LIVES?

Luke 13:12-17

And aren't we all pro-life? Maybe.
Or not. I can't decide.
Maybe the answer is sometimes,
for some lives.

It isn't a matter of for or against,
but of which.
Whose lives are worth saving—
pounding the pavement for in protest?

Or maybe the question is this:
life or profit?

Or, rather,
from which lives
will we profit?

Don't Despise Small Beginnings

Luke 13:18-21

My daughters, born prematurely,
and now the tallest in their first-grade class,
full of sass and all the Black Girl Magic
that six-year-old bodies can hold.

That small cup of stone-ground grits
turning into a pot large enough
to fill stomachs for days.
Please, hold the sugar, though.

The sit-in movement
that began with students
trained in church basements
became a revolution.

Eschatology

Luke 13:22-30

Waiting is a dangerous game.

Refusing to seize
    the opportunity when it's
        been presented has left me with

unintended consequences in the end.

The end—what do I make of it?

Does the run-on sentence
    of human history finish
        with terminal punctuation—

A period. A question mark? An exclamation!

Or does it continue on

behind the door of life
    that has been opened
        in this present moment—

a new set of words after a comma, or a semicolon?

This morning

the sun is rising
    over the East River

My children will wake in twenty minutes

The tulips outside my window
    unfolding upward
        after having made it through

the coldness of the night

Life is calling me, requesting

I embrace her nowness
    instead of waiting until
        the clock winds down

before I ask to dine at her table.

Ask Them Why

Luke 13:31

When they come
warning you
of government threats
against your body,
imploring you
to run and find cover
from the wrath
that will soon arrive,
ask them why
they are urging you
to get away
and not seeking
safe haven for themselves.
Ask them why
they remain in the realm
of good graces
and do not find themselves
in the crosshairs.

Foxes

Luke 13:32-35

I don't know much about farm life,
but I know that the fox
is the most feared chicken killer,

and I know that a mother hen
will do anything to protect
her chicks.

I learned this when my brother
was accused of stealing food
from a local Wawa,

and the boys in blue told the whole group
of us teenage Black boys we could never
step foot in that store again.

This happened
after they tracked us back
to our friend's house around the corner,

and forced my brother into a confession,
even though he had never been in
the Wawa that night.

When my mother found out
she drove straight down to the store
looking for the woman who lied about what happened.

She was the cashier, and she hid in the back
refusing to own up
to what she had done.

When the cops arrived again
she admitted she had lied about the yogurt.
When they left

she returned to her cash register
filling up her hours
until it was time to clock out for the night.

A LAMENT FOR THE
PROPHETS WE'VE KILLED

Luke 13:34-35

Our responsibility is to tell you the truth. But since you were
never told the truth, you will believe it a lie. Lies are more
affectionate than truth and embrace with both arms.
ROBERT JONES JR., *THE PROPHETS*

There is a lineage of those whose blood fills the streets
of cities and countrysides—prophets who have spoken truth
only to find their lips kissed with the blunt force
of thrown stones. They knew their end before they began,
and still they continued. Fire in the bones cannot be contained.
Handcuffs and shackles cannot restrain their message.
More than by their shouts, we know them by their tears—
salt dried on their cheeks from years of endless weeping.
Many of their names have been swept away by the winds
of history. It is the winners who write the accounts,
yet the ground bears witness.

VI

DINNER GUEST

Thanksgiving Etiquette

Luke 14:1

Ensure everyone is able
to stuff their faces
without giving thought
to kids in cages.

Do not dare utter the word *Native*.
Our fond memories of
Schoolhouse Rock
must remain intact.

Do not mention
that video:
we do not have
all the facts.

Please do not speak
about lack of healthcare:
today is a time
for gratitude.

This is our unspoken pact—
the law and order
of how we act
at all family gatherings.

LEX ET ORDO

Luke 14:2-6

Latin, meaning
control the ratchet—
the ones who act up
when life is snatched from us.

This is no dog whistle,
simply a signal
to contain the brutes,
tame the uncouth.

We have brought the healers
to heel,
concealed our intentions
under *lex et ordo*.

BREAKING

Luke 14:7

There is nothing like a story
to change the mood—to break or break open
the atmosphere of a room.

We used to say *break a left* or *break a right*
meaning turn now,
change direction without hesitation.

Instead of yelling imperatives,
he prefers the narrative method—
character development is his strong suit.

I wonder:

How will he write me?
How will he break me?

Saint Coltrane

Luke 14:8-11

For John Coltrane,
venerated as a saint within the African Orthodox Church

In 1966, Coltrane was invited to tour Japan
with his quintet. As guests in the land
they were treated like dignitaries. John was
even given a complimentary alto saxophone
to blow, except that he was known for tenor,
but tender hearts do not make demands when
asked to dine at another's table. He worked
the alto into his plans, even though he had
reached the point of holding his hand over
his liver. No one would have blamed a dying
legend for refusing to change course. But
legends do not become saints by insistence
on their own way.

WITH STRINGS ATTACHED

Luke 14:12-14

Strings are things we attach
when we want something back
—a return on the investment
of what we at times call love.
I'm just insuring my future assets,
like when I invited them to my wedding
expecting to find a card on the gift table
with a hefty sum and some words about
the future and blessings from God
that I won't take time to read;
then there's that cousin and their plus one
who I know won't bring nothin'
but will be sure to ask if they can take home leftovers
even though this is no buffet.
Truth is, I only sent them an invitation
because you asked me to.

I Am a Conflict-Free Zone

Luke 14:15

conflict, like smoke, around me
sucking the air
till there's none left to breathe

dinner is no place
for dispute. I reach
for anything

I find
a platitude to extinguish
the situation

hoping to
clear
the air between us,

like I learned from my dad
a disciple in the classroom
of conflict avoidance.

I just want to enjoy my plate
and not face
the faces around the table.

WE ALL EAT

Luke 14:16-24

How many promises have been made, saying
When I make it, we all eat.

Like a point guard making sure
his whole squad gets love in the box score.

Like LeBron James
coming through in the Klutch for his friends.

Like all of us
who have wanted to change our peoples' fortunes.

Who knew this was God talk?
We knew.

And we have receipts of all the excuses
from those who wouldn't ride with us in rough times.

Don't come knocking
when it's time to dine with us.

THESE BAGS

Luke 14:25-33

These bags I carry, I hold them dear. They are full of things near to my heart—things I have earned, things I have learned, things I have loved. I carry what I've inherited, cherishing what my parents have bequeathed to me—ways of being that I thought were all my own. My tone of speech, the way I process grief, what I use to relieve the pain. The warmth I feel when I recall the voice of my mother calling me by my nickname. I carry my genesis with me.

• • •

There are bags I have since added along the way—
the contents of which I would rather not name.
I shoulder this shame with me wherever I go.

My bags remain with me.
I never sit them down.
I keep a close eye on them
when strangers are around.

But long is the road,
and the cost of carrying
is far more
than the cost of letting go.

Salty Ghazal

Luke 14:34-35

When we show up we always bring extreme flavor.
That's my people—cut us, and we bleed flavor.

Mommas and aunties always season heavy,
just look at that plate and you can see flavor.

Bring some bland mac and cheese to the cookout,
you might hear someone shout, *Who brought this? It needs flavor!*

Heavy-handed with the salt, pepper, Lawry's—
pardon me, but I learned to be free with flavor.

Momma said *If you follow this recipe,*
you can guarantee flavor.

She always made her dishes with love,
put her foot in it—that's, indeed, flavor.

She named me Drew, a child of the aromatic—
the offspring of One who breeds flavor.

VII

FOUND

For the Ones Called Lost

Luke 15:1-2

I have been called lost,
gone astray
tossed by the waves
of the sea
A lost cause, meaning
hopeless,
destined
for Sheol
The land of no living
no light
like the darkness
of my skin
The melanated man
who wants
freedom
is a heretic
Out of step
in this
critical race
of faith
But lost causes
like Confederate lies
are myths
they do not exist
If lost means
I am
not found
in your company
Then I am right
where I
want
to be

THIS SIDE OF THE PASTURE

Luke 15:3-7

How could I blame
a sheep
for leaving
the flock

                        when the grass
                 on this side of the pasture
                          is so lush,
                          so green

                and there is no way to see
                  that those leafy blades
                 live so close to the edge
                     of the ravine—

                        so near
                  to where the wolves
              keep watch over the flock
                      by night.

     I too
     am prone to wander,
     enticed by the bright colors
     of these wildflowers.

And through my wandering
will I flower
into knowing
my foundness?

For what is it   to be lost   when every place I graze   is God's pasture?

To Be Still Is to Be Found

Luke 15:8-10

When I sit still at my kitchen counter
sipping wine in between exchanges of laughter
with a friend,

what circles around me?

I feel the brush of wind it creates
as it swirls—
in the eye of its storm.

And later, lying motionless on my sofa,
eyes closed, listening to Coltrane's breath
pass through his saxophone

I notice the zephyr again.

This time it settles on my chest—
saying something,
making its way around me.

There Is a Great Joy That Waits

Luke 15:9-10

Don't you hear the sound,
even if faintly?
I have gathered my friends.

PRODIGAL

Luke 15:11-13

prodigal /ˈprädəgəl/

1. spending money or resources freely and recklessly; wastefully
   extravagant.
2. having or giving something on a lavish scale

> adjective, usually
> a descriptor of someone
> who lacks wisdom
> acts improvident
> with what
> they've been given
>
> a spendthrift
> who liberally lavishes
> the world with beauty
> and is loose-handed
> with love
>
> and this
> is the image
> we are made in—
> who could blame
> a daughter or son
> for such wasteful
> behavior

GIVE ME MY SHARE

Luke 15:12

Give me the world—
    with all of its joys,
        withholding nothing.

I will not settle for someday,
    I will not wait
        for my pleasure.

Give me the full measure
    of Your cup
        that runneth over.

Goodness and mercy should be mine.
    I will go buy them
        at the market of satisfaction.

Give me passion
    and the freedom
        to make rash decisions.

Give me forgiveness
    when I return with nothing left
        but despair.

Give me my share—
    all that belongs to me.
        I am a rightful heir.

DISTANT COUNTRY

Luke 15:13

I do not know where I am going.
I do not need to know,
as long as it is far away from here—
nowhere near
your house of judgment.

> I am fed up with
> being forced to fit
> within your
> box.

I need the endless horizon.
I need the freedom to fail on my terms,
the experience of being hurt
and helped by strangers
who do not care that I am covered
in the dirt of yesterday's mistakes.
How can I learn to be me
living under this roof
where the number one rule
is that I must be you?

BRINK

Luke 15:13-16

There is an end
to myself
that I have reached.

A periphery
to my being
that I have met.

At this edge
I have nothing left
to give.

On the verge
of being swept
away like chaff.

How
ungodly
I am!

Walking.
Standing.
Sitting.

On this cliff,
small patches
of crabgrass growing.

The air here
is dense
with regret.

So many things
I would not
have known

had I not
made this trip
to my brink.

When I Came to Myself

Luke 15:17

when I finally   stopped   running

embraced
by the thought   of Love

when I had   enough   of being
separate

severed

weary of learning   lessons
weary

quit with   arguments of
unfairness

I escaped   my escape

Rehearsal

Luke 15:18-19

I believe worth
is determined   by work
    or to say
by how I play
my role.   I will return
    to the character
you want me
to be.   I will rehearse
    my self
to perfection.
Submerged   in this script.
    Each inflection
well practiced.
Each line   delivered
home.

Where the Road and Sky Shake Hands

Luke 15:20-24

I always imagine my father,
poised, sitting
on the front porch
with his eyes fixed
on that point in the distance
where the road and sky shake hands.

I wonder if my father
has been sitting
in that poised position, listening
for each noise disrupting the silence,
fist gripped
at the thought of my departure.

I often muse on where my mother is
as my father sits, poised and waiting.
Maybe she is canvassing the neighborhood,
interrogating my friends
as to where I might be.

I am thinking about how my father
and mother will receive me
when the light of the sun at my back
creates a silhouette of my body.
Or have I already presumed too much.
Poised before unleashing a storm of wrath.
Waiting to wage holy war—the aftermath
being only fire and brimstone.

LIKE A SLAVE

Luke 15:25-32

Our crown has already been bought and paid
for. All we have to do is wear it.
JAMES BALDWIN

Bondage.
No thriving here.
Only surviving.

Or dying.

The death of my dignity.
Buried in the grave
of your incessant demands.

I have kept each one—
like a slave.

I have traded
my personhood
to keep your commands.

This is no ode.
You owe me.

VIII

ECONOMICS

RICH MAN

Luke 16:1

We've forgotten that a rich life consists fundamentally of serving others,
trying to leave the world a little better than you found it. We need the
courage to question the powers that be, the courage to be impatient with
evil and patient with people, the courage to fight for social justice.
CORNEL WEST

I've been around folks
    who would sell their souls
        to acquire the green.

They would put bodies
    under pavement to increase
        stocks, bonds, and mutual funds.

I've sat in classrooms
    with those who thought they were made
        in the image and likeness of Madoff.

Reflections of Mammon—
    mouths stammering
        about wealth enhancement.

SITUATION ETHICS

Luke 16:1-9

Albert J. Raboteau notes that "lying and deceit, normally considered
moral vices, were virtues to slaves in their dealings with whites."
This radical reversal in moral reasoning was fueled by the basic
conviction that the only morally appropriate response to the
deception and depravity of slaveholders was to make every
effort not to fulfill the ultimate objective of their efforts, that
is, to produce hard-working, honest, and submissive slaves.

CHERYL SANDERS, EMPOWERMENT ETHICS
FOR A LIBERATED PEOPLE

When I sit long enough with my bones, I discover stories. Like a paleontologist, I use the fine-haired brush of my intuition to uncover things I never knew existed. In my lineage are ancestors who lived by a different set of ethics. With ankles and wrists pressed against the chains of enslavement, they made decisions that some today might call questionable.

Question: Who sets the standard of morality? God? Whose god? The one who sovereignly ordained these chains?

Well, then. Back to these bones.

Booker T told a story about his mother waking him at midnight to eat a chicken secured from an *unknown source*. Of course, he meant the master. Mother could not fathom her children's mouths remaining empty while they feasted, up at the big house, on the food she had raised.

We call God immutable, which usually means we refuse to change our view of God. Let every deception be in service of heaven.

Interrogating Mammon

Luke 16:10-13

There is a reason, after all, that some people wish to colonize the
moon, and others dance before it as before an ancient friend.
James Baldwin

How big is a billion?
What is its equivalent in lives?

How many bodies does it take
to reach the edge of outer space?

How do you face yourself each morning
with hands covered in blood?

How does it feel to have stacks
built on the bent backs of servitude?

What is it like to float on yachts
in your sea of green?

What is it like to see only green
in everything living and breathing?

Do you know what it feels like to breathe?
Do you know what it feels like to be alive?

Can you save us?
Can you send down fire to raze this field of iniquity?

Should we cut ourselves and scream to see if you hear us?
Are you asleep?

For the Love

Luke 16:14-18

My congregation,
full of dead men.
How I love them:

Benjamin
Ulysses
Andrew

Alexander
Abraham
George

I forage the Scriptures
for a word that will meet them
where they are

Cue the worship band
to play
"O Come to the Altar."

I count them
carefully,
saying their names.

WISHES

Luke 16:19-21

I see him when I walk
 across 14th street.
  Feet sticking out

from under
 another's
  throwaway blanket.

Crusted over.
 Gangrene. Sneaker store
  in my peripheral vision

that, to him, likely
 seems a lifetime away—
  a great gulf fixed.

I slip my hand
 into my pocket
  to assuage my guilt.

I wish I could
 fill his hands
  with cash.

I wish I could
 fill my heart
  with compassion.

I wish I could
    fill my mouth
        with courage

to ask his name . . .

I wish I could
    see him as
        more than a barrier

on my way to the L train.

MTA card
    in my hand
        I push the gate open.

Dog Spells God Backwards

Luke 16:21

Every day, leaned up against the wall of Target,
there he sits with man's best friend.
One to keep him company
while every other being
in this city that remains asleep
cannot be bothered
to cut our eyes in his direction.

I have never asked the question
if God could put on flesh
in the form of a K-9.
But if the rocks can cry out,
no doubt the dogs can be a disguise
for the God who is a friend
that sticks closer than a brother.

THRESHOLD

Luke 16:22-26

Listen to me, I want a single bill from you
Nothin' less, nothin' more
I told him I ain't have it and closed my door
Tell me how much a dollar cost.

KENDRICK LAMAR, "HOW MUCH A DOLLAR COST"

Every step over bodies lying at the gate
is a step into the dark abyss—
a stride into a lifeless wasteland
that is its own kind of torment.

This is a threshold
crossed only by those
who spend their days
trying to gain the world.

What if hell is not a place
where lost souls go—
no nine circles
of inferno,

but a home
constructed by those
with no soul
at all?

What if the soul vanishes
when it chases
after nothing
but the wind?

WHEN THE PROPHETS COME

Luke 16:27-31

We ought to come in mule carts, in old trucks, any kind of transportation
people can get their hands on. People ought to come to Washington,
sit down if necessary in the middle of the street and say,
"We are here; we are poor; we don't have any money; you have made us
this way . . . and we've come to stay until you do something about it."
MARTIN LUTHER KING JR.

When the prophets come
they will show up
holding signs that read:

I AM
A MAN.

They will make
demands
to not be treated like
sanitation.

They will campaign
to the point
of assassination.

When the prophets come
we
will assassinate them
like we always do

whether it be
with
a bullet
a crucifixion

or
a refusal
to look them
in the eye
as we pass them by
on the road.

IX

KINGDOM COME

STUMBLING BLOCKS

Luke 17:1-2

I was a young Black boy. I cannot recall how old. But I do recall the older white man's grin as he stood over me on the back steps of the church, threatening to *get his hood out of the trunk of his car* if I did not sharpen my behavior. Iron sharpens iron, I guess. The next time, out in the parking lot, he looked at me and said *smile so I can see you.* Wearing the same grin. I wonder if it was then that the thought grew in me that I needed to shed my blackness in order to be seen by God—to receive the blood that was shed for me. White as snow.

I heard about stumbling blocks at church. Usually from some man warning us boys to avoid the girls in spaghetti straps and skirts above the knee. We were told they were a trap. That and rap music. Any bad action we took could be blamed on the traps and on the black music.

BE ON GUARD

Luke 17:3

My guardian angel
greets me in the night—
a welcome sight
for the one trembling
at the thought of becoming
what caused me harm.
I say to my angel:
Please guard me from malformation.
My angel replies:
That is your job.

IF ANOTHER DISCIPLE SINS

Luke 17:3

diminishes the Image in another
refuses to be a keeper of a brother
or sister
ignores our kin in prison
withholds compassion
is rash with words
strings nouns and verbs together
to hurt instead of heal
conceals the truth
steals people from their home nation
makes them labor on plantations
privileges the world for racists
and rapists
scoffs when we are forced to face this
carnage
harms. harms. harms.
we are in the wrong
if we don't
give them hell

PINE-SOL AND GOSPEL MUSIC

Luke 17:3-4

My Black mom loved gospel music.
There was no feeling like
hearing Tramaine Hawkins

sing about the potter's house
as our house filled with the aroma
of Pine-Sol for Saturday morning cleaning.

I remember Helen Baylor singing
about the *Sea of Forgetfulness*
and seventy times seven of the refrain.

Such abundance.
Such forgiveness.
Even then I wondered:

How could I practice this
when I'd already learned
the habit of resentment.

How can someone be repentant
if they have to keep asking
for the same thing?

Do I have to forgive
if they don't change their mind
about their hatred of my skin?

Every Living Thing
Was Once a Seed

Luke 17:5-6

Every living thing was once a seed.
This poem.
That daisy.
Faith.

Small, yet determined
to crack the unbelieving earth—
dirt, like us.

I have never been a fan of mustard.
Too bitter, aftertaste lingers
on my tongue.

My taste buds prefer something sweeter—
easier than the biting flavor of waiting
on my trust in the way of love to grow.

GOLD STAR

Luke 17:7-10

The tree blooms in season
with no expectation of receiving applause
for bearing fruit.

It does not hang its branches,
dragging its hands in the dirt
when the earth does not sing its praises,
when the sky does not lie prostrate
at its roots.

When we have done what is ours to do
there is no use
in waiting around
for a gold star.

For I Am Like Jonah

Luke 17:11-13

I see them in the distance.
Group of ten. Stench
of rotting flesh
accosting my nostrils,
causing them to curl heavenward.

Heaven likely heard
my groan—
a reaction I learned
from those older
who had passed this way before.

I quickly change my face,
shapeshift,
deadpan,
so as to not attract
attention.

Muscle tension increases
as I see their eyes rise
in our direction.
I expect to hear the words
Unclean! Unclean!

But instead they shout
Mercy!
Everything in me
recoils at the thought,
for I am like Jonah.

KINDNESS TRAVELS

Luke 17:11-13

Every public floor contains those dots
that indicate
        6 ft apart.

Keep your distance!

It seems we have not figured out
how to make kindness travel
the length of the gap

                    between   us.

Roses for God

Luke 17:14-15

Silent gratitude isn't very much use to anyone.
GERTRUDE STEIN

The last time someone turned back
they were turned into a pillar
of salt.

It is enough to feel gratitude
in my heart,

though I do appreciate
when words of gratefulness
come my way.

They say
God knows your heart,

but maybe even God
likes to receive roses.

The Faces of the Blessed

Luke 17:16-19

I guess blessing means entitlement.
I have been told my birthright is a curse.

    My birthright, to be cursed because of genetics.
    Ethnicity determines my access to healing.

I am right to think healing will pass me by
as it has done before in the faces of the blessed.

    The faces of the blessed expect the world.
    Anything less is an affront.

It is an affront to turn and say *thank you*—
an insult to show gratitude for what is rightfully theirs.

    Rightfully theirs, they are the rightful heirs
    of every privilege of mercy.

Privileged to receive mercy, I say *thank you.*
I guess blessing means entitlement.

THE KINGDOM OF TREES

Luke 17:20-21

*The trees soon revealed startling secrets. I discovered that they are
in a web of interdependence, linked by a system of
underground channels, where they perceive and connect
and relate with an ancient intricacy and wisdom.*

SUZANNE SIMARD

To say that I am within the trees
is to say that I am among them.
The trees consider themselves
a collective, connected at the root.
Communicating through mycelium,
sharing generational wisdom.
They do not withhold,
there is no competition—
always and ever giving.
And we marvel at how the trees seem
to live forever—
this never-ending kingdom.

ORDINARY DAYS

Luke 17:22-30

Ordinary days are for dreamers.
Those mundane days
where time fades away

faster than the color of my new t-shirt
after running it through
the washing machine.

Ordinary days
where plates are washed clean
after dinners of cornbread,
fried chicken, and collard greens.

They call me a daydreamer—
like Lot, like Noah—
seeing a future of fire and flood

while we sit around, running
our mouths like we always do.
Passing the time of these lazy days.

No sense
of impending doom.

Remember Lot's Wife

Luke 17:31-36

She meant to look away, but the sting in her eyes held her there.
Natalie Diaz, "Of Course She Looked Back"

Natalie Diaz said that I would have too—
looked back at my smoldering city,
the embers of what was once my home.

I'd like to talk about blame.
The way we so quickly name something as wrong
before facing the situation
of becoming a pillar of salt.

Maybe she was the first to be salt of the earth.
Maybe hers were tears of blessed mourning.
Maybe this pillar is a memorial.

Maybe.

May we carefully attend
to the way we remember.
Presumption can be
a deadly disease.

AETOS

Luke 17:37

Could also be translated as *eagle*.
Aquila. Gold standard. Carried into battle
by Roman legions.

    We do not have to ask
    if there is any significance
    to the symbols we choose.

Aspirational, they tell us
who we want to be—
how we see ourselves.

    World conquerors,
    gathering around humans
    soon to be corpses.

Small countries.
Black and brown bodies.
A delicacy.

X

MERCY

THE VIRTUE OF ANNOYANCE

Luke 18:1-8

There's a line about a squeaky wheel.
I wonder if persistence

is just another name for annoyance.
Did we annoy our way to the end of segregation?

Nevertheless, she was annoying?

I guess it's still justice
if people are just fed up with us:

perturbed by the sound of our voices.
Annoyance is a virtue.

When Hatred Goes to Church

Luke 18:9-12

Hatred likes to
disguise itself
as gratitude.
Dress itself
in a three-piece suit.
Use religious verbiage.
Turn amens
into stamps
of approval
on bigotry.
Thanking
Thanking
Thanking
God that I am not
like them.
And the church said,
amen.

FACING HEAVEN

Luke 18:13-14

I wish humility
was not the child of humiliation—

did not nurse
at the breast of rejection.

I wish heaven knew
what my face looked like.

That is to say,
I long to face the sky

with something akin
to confidence.

BLOCKING BLESSING

Luke 18:15

The true character of a society is revealed in how it treats its children.
NELSON MANDELA

We block the children
from blessing
and call it God's work.

Keeping God's hand
from extending
toward the lead-filled
water of Flint.

Raising the number
of prison beds
instead of the level
of education.

Stifling imagination,
determining lives on the basis
of a correctly filled-in
scantron bubble.

Calling in the badges
for every "bad kid"
who was looking for love
but instead found trouble.

Native children
buried under
boarding school rubble—
forgotten history.

EVEN INFANTS

Luke 18:15-17

And what do infants do
but sleep, except
when they are waking
with cries of
feed me, feed me.

What do infants do
but take, or, rather,
receive what is given.

They are not foolish.
They have not yet been duped
into believing that life is independent.

And is this the arc of life?
To end up back where we started?
Do we depart only to return?
Is this the new birth?

What Must I Do?

Luke 18:18-25

As if Life is something I can earn.
Intern my way
up
    the
        ladder.

Add it to my resume
right above Master
of Divinity.

As if I can add Life to my stack
of achievements.
Pile it on top
of these degrees.

I let go of everything
I'm holding on to
for dear life.

Mortally Impossible

Luke 18:26-30

We're like merchants,
hoping to purchase our way to God's new world.

Like ships crossing the Atlantic
with human cargo,

with no embargo on this trade.
We've betrayed and become traitors

to one another, and the possibility of love
floats away.

COMPREHENSION

Luke 18:31-34

Part of being a student is
> *not understanding.*

I dropped Calculus
with the quickness
because derivatives
vectors and limits
were foreign language
even after
> One
>
> Two
>
> Three

explanations.
No charm here.
I still
> *comprehend nothing.*

What Do You Want Me to Do for You?

Luke 18:35-43

And that is the question.
The quest of life—
restless searching for this answer.

I want cancer gone
so that it does not steal my mother.

Cancer stole my mother.
What do I want other than her return?

I will return to the question at hand.
I will come back to my restless heart.

I want hearts to grow warm,
slowly, like my hands after
a cold night walking through my city.

My city, I want it free
of bodies warming on sidewalk grates.

Or is this what I'm supposed to say?

I want to know
what my heart wants.

XI

REPARATION

WEE LITTLE MAN

Luke 19:1-3

Strange, the way the past
never stays where it came from.

Shows up again
    and
       again.

Something must've bludgeoned
    my shoulder.
A repeating pain.

Tree Climbing

Luke 19:3-4

And isn't there always something

    in
    the
    way.

Call it a crowd.
Call it the loud preacher
screaming me into hell.
Call it the friend
who tells me I've strayed.
Call it the way faith
has been manipulated—
the gap
between doctrine and love.

Observe how
each obstruction
piles up.

    One
    on
    top
    of
    the
    other.

And watch the way
they blame me
for my inability
to see.

I Think It Was Brunch

Luke 19:5-7

I often wonder about that dinner
Or was it lunch?
One asked the other
if he preferred coffee black or with cream.
Steam rose from the cups.
Laughter filled the space between them.

How was the ice broken?
Jesus tells a joke about a rabbi
and a tax collector.

They exchanged glances.
One man scanning the room
the other looking back.
How long did it take for water
to pool in their bottom lids?
What was said before the first
tear hit the table?

I wonder what word enabled
a closed-off heart and a tight-fisted hand
to open so wide?
Or was a word even necessary?
Maybe presence is all it took.
Maybe presence is all that was ever needed.

No Repentance Without Repair

Luke 19:8-10

*It is as though we have run up a credit-card bill and, having pledged to
charge no more, remain befuddled that the balance does not disappear.
The effects of that balance, interest accruing daily, are all around us.*

Ta-Nehisi Coates, "The Case for Reparations"

And I will tell you what repentance looks like for America:
pay back. No, not the vengeance America holds dear—

> *We will not forgive.*
> *We will not forget.*
> *We will hunt you down and make you pay.*

It looks like repayment. Recompense for everything stolen.
Where to begin? The beginning is as good a place as any—
a kleptocracy since inception. Since those ships set sail west
and laid claim to lands already inhabited. Then sailed back
across the Atlantic to capture bodies inhabited by the soul
of Africa. This nation built on the backs of my ancestors who
received lashes instead of cash for their work. And when freedom
promised 40 acres and a mule, America stole that too. Redistributed
to the hands of former Confederates who went on to build
generational wealth. And we got dealt the terror of the Klan—
those hooded white knights determined to beat back any
advances we made. We watched plantations turn to prisons.
We watched Tulsa burn. We were beat up and shot down
just to earn our basic rights. Denied the benefits of the G.I. Bill
after fighting on the front lines. We were redlined out of houses.
Huddled into ghettos. Then thrown bags of crack for our troubles.

No, a simple *I'm sorry* will not do.
A banner reading *Black Lives Matter* will not suffice.
For salvation to visit this house
America must dish out
far more than it can afford.

THE WAITING GAME

Luke 19:11-27

Waiting
    for the sun to rise
    and fall each day, taking
    the light away with it.

Waiting
    for winter—
    that cold space of deadness—
    to overtake once again.

Waiting
    for war, the next nation
    declaring its intent
    to destroy.

Waiting
    to be let down again—
    failed as I have been
    before.

Waiting
    for the other shoe
    to drop
    as I know it will.

Waiting
    for breath to spill
    out of my lungs
    one final time.

Waiting
to be found
while hiding
from everything I've been
waiting for.

PART II

JERUSALEM

XII

Triumph

BEAST OF BURDEN

Luke 19:28-35

After Mary Oliver's "The Poet Thinks About the Donkey"

They say the donkey is
a beast of burden.

Its purpose—
to carry heavy loads.

And did this donkey know
the weight it carried?

The hopes and fears of all the years
on the back of this young colt.

The young have always carried
the burdens of the future.

HOSANNA

Luke 19:36-38

A cry of liberation
from the lips of those
who do not wish to maintain
the status quo—
a longing for Babylon,
America, and Rome
to be overthrown.

Could our *hosannas* go deeper?
Cut off the root
of an empire's fruit?

Singing Rocks

Luke 19:39-40

While it seems like the high iron content . . . is the reason why the rocks ring, it's really something else. What we're hearing isn't the sound of metal, but the sound of tension . . . stress gauges showed that their inner materials were under considerable strain.

Esther Inglis-Arkell, "Listen to the Strange Phenomenon of 'Singing Stones'"

Under great strain
the rocks let out their freedom song.
Haven't we always done this?
Make music out of pain?

Chuck Berry took that rock
and made it into a new genre.
B. B. let it ring
through the strings of Lucille.

And still we could not hear it.
Frequencies outside our sonic range.

THE LAST FRONTIER

Luke 19:41-44

I walked down Avenue D
and wandered into the Jacob Riis Houses.
They call them projects, from the Middle English *projecte*,
meaning a plan, a scheme, a design. Something
intentionally crafted in the mind. I wind through
the concrete sidewalks which create a maze
of sorts between the brick and metal edifices.
Evidence of the city's neglect all around me—
overgrown weeds where children once played
hopscotch. Backboards with no rims attached.
Cracked pavement as far as the eye can see. I see
two women sitting on a bench, deep in conversation.
Walking by I say hello and of course they invite
me to sit. Hospitality is a characteristic of heaven.
Sensing that I'm new they begin to tell me all
about the neighborhood. Squatters in low rises.
Riots at Tompkins. The years of Mayor Koch
which brought rising racial tension. But one thing
sticks out:

We've been pushed to the edge here.
We call this the last frontier.

Welcome to the neighborhood.
We're glad you're here.

FLIPPING TABLES

Luke 19:45-48

Sometimes
I need to flip
tables
not concern
myself
with whether
there's space for me
to sit.

XIII

QUESTIONS

Haiku: Unanswered

Luke 20:1-8

Oh, it feels so good
to show up and just do me—
owing no answers!

BEAUTIFUL REJECTION

Luke 20:9-19

And we have learned
there is nothing so beautiful
as rejection.

Unwanted animal scraps
discarded by our enslavers
taken and turned
into soul food.

Richard Allen and Absalom Jones
rejected from those Methodist pews,
constructing an ecclesial movement
of ebony and mahogany.

The story of Michael Jordan
being cut from his high school team
became legendary to us—
the way he built that into 6 rings.

There are rejected things inside of me.
I will one day uncover
only to remold
into poetry.

MACHINATIONS

Luke 20:20

I have always liked the word

                machination.

I'm fascinated by how it rolls

                off the tongue.

How it first has to gather in the back

                of the throat

Behind the closed doors of my teeth

                in secret

Plotting how it will make its way

                into the next sentence

Its entrance undetected, unsuspectedly

                arresting me

With its charm.

GIVE TO CAESAR

Luke 20:21-26

What inscription, whose image has been
pressed and printed on these coins,
this paper?

If the faces
are an indication,
who is this god
in whom we trust?

We pay tribute
to powder-wigged,
pale-skinned
men, then
pray they give us this day
new roadways
and social safety nets.

Blessed be the god
and founding fathers?

In the Age to Come

Luke 20:27-44

There will be no edges, but curves.
Clean lines pointing only forward.
TRACY K. SMITH, "SCI-FI"

Every relationship redefined.
Definition is no fixed thing;
it changes
with the ages, eons, epochs.
We cannot
bring our well-defined boxes
with us where we are going.
Like coffins
they are meant for death.
Everything ahead of us
is alive.

For the Sake of Appearance

Luke 20:45-47

The word that comes to mind is *manicure*.
The way I spent the weekends of my youth
waiting for hours to get lined up

at Doc's Barbershop. Only certain hands
could touch this head. Steady.
I must impress.

I took every chance I had
to grab new gear at the
Deptford Mall or Franklin Mills.

Now years later I spend my weekends
tending to my sermons. Trimming
each edge, dressing to impress.

XIV

WARNINGS

Butterscotch Hard Candy

Luke 21:1-4

I knew she had very little,
but every visit she would
slip me a few dollars
to put in my wallet.

She always added
a butterscotch hard candy.

The sound of her
clutch snapping shut
still echoes.

Building Campaign

Luke 21:5-6

I know it well—the vision given. A picture of the future building placed
    in the foyer
so all who enter can glimpse how enormous it will be. Then come the
    slogans:

Building something eternal.
More than bricks.
Making a place to gather and grow.

Each week, show the progress—how many checks have come in. How
much the congregation has promised to invest in the house of the Lord.

Cue the sermon. Psalm 127.
Unless the Lord builds the house . . .

I think about my mother's house,
how she built it with love—
such materials that moth and rust
cannot corrupt.

She needed no campaign
to construct a place big enough
for God to dwell.

Before It All Ends

Luke 21:7-24

When you expect the world to end at any moment,
you know there is no need to hurry.
You take your time, you do your work well.
THOMAS MERTON

I have already lived
through several ends of the world.

The History Channel
filled with
Nostradamus documentaries

as the year 2000
drew near.

Dissecting the Mayan calendar—
no errors
in our calculations.

Billboards paid for
by Harold Camping
lining the interstate.

Imminence

Luke 21:9

When I heard of it
on January 6th
I was terrified.

Although crosses
and nooses
used for the sake of
intimidation
in the name of Jesus
are things
I have seen before.

Perhaps
this familiarity
is where the dread
came from.

We have always known
that the end
is imminent.

How could we not?

When the Powers of Heaven Shake

Luke 21:25-28

I have existed from the morning of the world and I shall exist
until the last star falls from the night. Although I have taken
the form of Gaius Caligula, I am all men as I am
no man and therefore I am a God.
CALIGULA, EMPEROR OF ROME

Historical facts regarding
the collapse of Rome:

incompetent emperors
climate change
disease epidemics
a weakened army
a crumbling economy.

Beside these things,
the myth began to lose its power.

Sometimes Death Comes

Luke 21:29-33

Fall in the northeast is a thing of beauty.
A flood of color covers the Appalachians.
We watch the leaves slowly leave behind
their green, embracing shades of

                       yellow
                       orange
                       red.

Sometimes death comes
    warning us
    of its arrival.

N. Y. State of Mind

Luke 21:34-38

I never sleep, cause sleep is the cousin of death.

Nas, "N. Y. State of Mind"

Vigilance is essential
when living in this Big City of Dreams,
where schemers plot and
Citi bikers never stop
for the walkers.

Horns will certainly honk
if you're not paying attention
the second the light turns
from red to green.

Pickpockets still roam the streets
around Times Square.

Watch out for the dudes
who claim to be Uber at the airport
but do not sport
the black and white U in their windows.

And of course remain alert
on the subway.
You do not want to ride the A train
and miss all 59 stops
ending up in Far Rockaway.

XV

PASSION

30 Pieces

Luke 22:1-6

I think he was sorry he did what he did. He thought the FBI
was only going to raid the house. But the FBI gave it over
to the state's attorney and that was all Hanrahan wanted.
They shot Fred Hampton and made sure he was dead.

Ben Heard, Uncle of Bill O'Neal,
FBI Informant in the Assassination
of Fred Hampton

Intentional scheme—
to offer a poor man
30 pieces.

Upper Room

Luke 22:7-13

Now I'm in the upper room
Talking with my Lord
Yes, and your God.
Mahalia Jackson,
"In the Upper Room"

There is a room
ready and furnished,
awaiting preparation
for us.

There is a room—
Ms. Mahalia knew it well;
there she serenaded Martin
in his despair.

There is a room
where we will share bread—
dining together
face to face.

There is a room
in the place
where you are.

Eucharisteo

Luke 22:14-16

A table prepared before me
in the presence of
friends and enemies
deserters and betrayers.

The ones with edges
sharp as stones,
cleaning the bones
of this lamb roast.

Brothers
with thunder in their guts—
rumbling anger,
loud as hunger pains.

My beloved
whose head I hold
close to my chest,
breath smelling
of bitter herbs.

This Is My Body

Luke 22:17-19

All bread must be broken
so it can be shared. Together
we eat this earth.
Margaret Atwood, "All Bread"

There is nothing so abundant
and yet so withheld.

Grocery shelves spill with this
wonder.

Stomachs rumble everywhere, wondering
where the bread is.

So many varieties other than white,
which has no nutritional value,

yet somehow is most often found
in the cupboards of the poor.

Give me the bread that looks like
it's spent some time in the sun—

like melanin has risen to the surface
of its dough.

This is my body.
This is all bodies.

THIS CUP

Luke 22:20-23

After Psalm 75:8

In the hand of the Lord there is a cup
of foaming wine, well mixed;

and what is in this cup?
Is it the blood of sinners, crushed
in the hands of this angry god,

who foams at the mouth, rabid,
ready to attack the unsuspecting
and those who don't quote
the doctrine of his choosing
quite correctly?

Is it the preferred drink of theologians
who insist on certain theories of atonement
but are willing to own and condone
the enslavement of my people?

Or maybe it is a cup foaming over
with cabernet-colored love

And all the wicked of the earth
shall drain it down to the dregs.

Towel and Basin

Luke 22:24-27

He knew he was a king. His mother used to tell him
every morning at daybreak.

Never forget it.

The wet mop slapped the floor,
cleaning the spilled tea
of one who could afford
to live
in the building.

We need our caffeinated liquid.

He was meticulous with his work.
Never leaving a trace
of the accidents
we walked away from.

His whistling filled the lobby.
His smile brighter
than the yellow signs
cautioning us
of wet floors.

The Kingdom Is Ours

Luke 22:28-30

Does the king make a kingdom?
Or does a kingdom make a king?
This hidden empire of kings and queens, that no one's noticing
Lupe Fiasco and Damian Marley, "Kingdom"

This is what we have been granted, my loves.
Heaven and earth have met
and they have met in us.

We are the ones—
the wretched of the earth.
The worth of the cosmos resounding
in our bodies.

Stardust.
What we have been given
cannot be shaken,
cannot be taken away.

For it has been conferred, confirmed
by the blood that courses
through our veins.
The DNA test returned positive.

We are the heirs.
We are the air
that will fill the new creation
with glorious breath.

We are
what comes next.

Sifted

Luke 22:31-34

Wheat is not ready for use
until it has been sifted—
spread out on the threshing floor
and beaten
until the chaff shows itself
for what it is.

The chaff is lightweight,
easily blown away by the breeze.
The wheat winnowed down until
all that remains is the grain of life,
soon to become bread for the world.

Two Swords

Luke 22:35-38

The Second Amendment—cold, cruel,

a constitutional violence, a ruthless

thing worrying me still.

REGINALD DWAYNE BETTS,
"WHEN I THINK OF TAMIR RICE
WHILE DRIVING"

Let's face it,
two swords could never be enough
for self-defense.

Certainly not enough
to go on the offensive.

He must've meant
two per person.

A well-regulated
militia.

A Stone's Throw

Luke 22:39-46

I watch as a vulture crosses over me, heading toward the carcasses
I haven't properly mourned or even forgiven.
What if, instead of carrying a child,
I am supposed to carry grief?

ADA LIMÓN, "THE VULTURE AND THE BODY"

Have you ever heard the sound of grief?
It wrenches the gut open—
twists and pulls until
every inner organ is exposed.

It cuts through the silence
with knife-like precision,
keeping solace at bay
with the tip of its blade.

It sounds like exhaustion;
like bodily fluids have been lost
on the ground—
sweat, tears, blood.

It sounds like thunder
and lightning crashing;
a storm of emotion brewing
into a hurricane of desire.

It sounds like white noise,
putting me to sleep.
I dream
as if it does not exist.

It sounds like a cry,
keep your distance—
a stone's throw away.

....

KISS OF DEATH

Luke 22:47-53

My Dad used to play "Back Stabbers"
by the O'Jays around the house—
the soundtrack of my youth.

Those ominous piano notes
let me know
that something was coming.

I listened as Eddie Levert
warned me about those friends
who show off their smiles,
and grace cheeks with kisses:

the blades are long,
clenched tight in their fists.
Aimin' straight at your back
and I don't think they'll miss.

What they do?

A question that leaves you
with nothing but suspicion.

Am I capable of giving
the kiss of death?

Peirasmos

Luke 22:54-62

I lost many things
in the flames
    that night.

    My sense of self.
    My life.

I died beside the fire.
I can no longer live in denial
of who I am.

The fire costs.

Dross bubbles to the surface.
Scraped away.

LIKE A KING

Luke 22:63-65

They mocked George Floyd,
spreading a meme throughout the LAPD that read
You take my breath away.
A funny valentine, I guess.

They mocked Eric Garner on a TV screen,
live behind a news reporter,
miming a chokehold, mouthing
I can't breathe.

They mocked the chokehold
of Elijah McClain.
Smiling while
standing in front of his memorial.

She wore a T-shirt
mocking the beating of Rodney that read,
L.A.P.D. We Treat You Like a King.
Later she became Philly's Commissioner of Police.

DEATH ROW TRIAL #1

Luke 22:66-71

*The intense pressure to obtain a death sentence and the political
stakes for police, prosecutors, and even judges can cause serious legal
errors that contribute to wrongful convictions and death sentences.*
EQUAL JUSTICE INITIATIVE

Pose question after
question
to get the innocent
to position himself
as guilty.

XVI

DEATH

Death Row Trial #2

Luke 23:1-5

The court had jurisdiction in debt and trespass where
the amount did not exceed 40 shillings.

THE HISTORICAL SOCIETY OF
THE NEW YORK COURTS,
THE PETTY COURT

We in this petty court
have no real power,
at least not to bring down
the magnitude of the conviction
we seek.

Out of our jurisdiction.
We bring in
the big guns.

The same ones
who have beaten us
into submission.

Let's trump up
the charges:

Perverting the nation
Tax evasion
Proclaiming himself king

By which we mean
he is seeking to spark a rebellion,
the hellion that he is.

Just ask J. Edgar Hoover.
He knows this trick well.

DEATH ROW TRIAL #3

Luke 23:6-12

Certain judges are known for their harshness,
and this one was
particularly draconian.

A hanging judge.
Go ask my headless cousin.

I can only think of my mother
whose son now stands before
the tyrant who took the life
of her precious nephew.

We leapt together in the womb.
I will likely see him again soon.

So much on my mind.
I can hardly
form a word.

DEATH ROW TRIAL #4

Luke 23:13-25

The death penalty is not about whether people deserve to die for the crimes they commit. The real question of capital punishment in this country is, do we deserve to kill?
BRYAN STEVENSON, *JUST MERCY*

We know
the powers will fold
if we put enough pressure on them.

In the end the goal is simple:
keep the people subdued.
Placation, one of their primary tools.

What if they kill because we let them?
What if they are just giving us what we want?

What if this
is what we want?

VIA CRUCIS:
SWEET BLACKNESS

Luke 23:26

For Simon of Cyrene, also believed to be Simeon
Niger, father of Rufus and Alexander

Cyrene.
Located in Northern Africa.
Eastern Libya.

Using African bodies
for manual labor—
a practice that is millennia old.

H. T. Johnson spoke of
The Black Man's Burden:
carrying the load of imperial supremacy.

Simon showed
that to bear this weight
is to carry the burden of God.

O, sweet blackness
that companions
the crucified!

O, beautiful darkness
that buoys
the burdened!

You, the first
to carry the cross
of discipleship.

VIA CRUCIS:
DAUGHTERS OF JERUSALEM

Luke 23:27-31

How long, how long?
When will the Daughters of Zion rejoice
In the house of the Lord?
THE PORTER'S GATE,
"DAUGHTERS OF ZION"

Surely they were there
drenching the road with tears.
Surely years of suffering had formed them
to run toward those in pain.

How could they run away
like their brothers?
The sting of abandonment
all too familiar to them.

I have seen the image of Mamie Till
wailing at her son's casket.
Her eyes pulled shut.
Her cheeks lifted up in agony.

I have seen the image of Lezley McSpadden.
Tears dripping down her brown-skinned face.
Her boy lay baking in the August sun,
sprawled across that Ferguson street.

Via Crucis:
Two Others

Luke 23:32, 39-43

For the two others, traditionally named Dismas and Gestas

I will not criminalize these two.
I do not know their crimes.
I do know they did not deserve to die.

And to die nameless
at the hands of the state,
staked to poles lowered into the ground.

I do know the state has a reputation
of crucifying
the innocent.

I do know that the word translated
robber
actually means
rebel.

Their story
turned into an allegory
about deathbed confession.

Forgive Them, Father

Luke 23:33-37

*We must become intentional about recognizing and embracing
our shadows. Religion's word for this is quite simply forgiveness,
which is pivotal and central on the path of transformation.*

RICHARD ROHR

What is it that we do not know?
   Do not let us off so easily
      with the charge of cluelessness.

Our aggression cannot be
   so easily dismissed.
      Neither can our oblivion.

We know what it is
   to dip our hands in blood.
      We know what it is

to witness such a thing
   and keep our mouths shut,
      saying nothing.

We know what it is,
   a cardinal sin, to abandon
      our friends when they're in need.

We have learned well
   the art of victim blaming.
      Shaming—our weapon of choice.

We are not innocent.
   We are part and parcel
      of this slaughter.

THE NINTH HOUR

Luke 23:44-49

I turned to my left,
my eyes swept across the terrain
to see if anyone had remained—
stayed close by while the noonday sky
filled with thick darkness.

I turned again, hoping
to find your right hand
that always beckoned me to come and sit,
but now my enemies have made me their footstool,
and you are nowhere to be found.

Listening for your voice,
but only hearing the pounding of my heart
and the sound of my bones being crushed
under the weight of this forsakenness.

I have known what it means
to be alone—at home,
silent and still, in the desert of my soul.

But this
is more than I
can bear.

Even my breath can't be near me,
slipping out of my lungs.
Rejecting me.

Like a seed, I fall
into the earth alone,
with nothing
but the stones
to keep me company.

Spectacle

Luke 23:48

In the "lynching era," between 1880 to 1940,
white Christians lynched nearly five thousand black men
and women in a manner with obvious echoes of the
Roman crucifixion of Jesus. Yet these "Christians"
did not see the irony or contradiction in their actions.

JAMES CONE, THE CROSS AND THE LYNCHING TREE

I don't know what is more jarring:
that these spectacles were turned into postcards
or that they took place in the front yard of the church.

There is an image that haunts me—
a sea of white faces posing for a photograph.
Smiling. Laughing.

One man points his bony finger
at the lynched bodies
with an obvious look on his face that says

This is what will happen to you, too.

It pains me to say this,
but I see myself in the man hanging on the right.
He looks like he could be my relative.

Maybe the other man does as well,
but I can hardly tell
given how disfigured he appears.

And I imagine that this happened
after dinner on the grounds,
after the sound of "The Old Rugged Cross"
faded into the night.

SATURDAY

Luke 23:50-56

Black folks have been locked into that long Saturday after Good Friday. We ain't had Easter yet. All we have is each other, and the promise of Easter, the promise of freedom.

CORNEL WEST, HOPE ON A TIGHTROPE

Liminal space—
betwixt and between—
when all I can see is loss.

I toss and turn in bed.
I dread
what tomorrow may hold.

I was told that gain is coming—
that after the rain
the sun will shine.

But my mind
can only conceive of death;
it is all we have ever known.

XVII

RESURRECTION

Under the Ground

Luke 24:1-12

In the beginning there is darkness. It is the womb out of
which we are born. . . . In this state of trusting refuge,
the light of divine revelation, which pierces but does not castigate
the darkness, may finally be seen.
This is a mothering darkness that nurses its offspring.
Dr. Barbara Holmes, Race and the Cosmos

Life is always happening
underground—
the place light has forsaken.

Finite minds cannot take in
that the belly of mother Earth
is, indeed, a womb.

Entombed in the soil is the pip
of a new Eden.
Only the seed that has fallen into the pit

can burst through into the morning dew
to announce to weeping eyes
that a new day has risen—

a day in which the voices and stories of women
are believed, their word received
as good news,

and the men have no problem
following them and
learning how to believe again.

What I mean is this:
the world has been flipped
on its head.

Heaven has invaded hell,
the spell of death is broken,
and the doorway opened to a new way of being.

It all begins with seeing
that the darkness of our world is luminous,
and in the humus of life is where we become

fully human.

EMMAUS

Luke 24:13-35

Making sense of tragedy is
an impossible task.
How do you shape meaning
out of the absurd?

There is a certain kind of hurt
that can only be comprehended
in the context of friendship,
over bread broken.

Those hours after the funeral
at the repast I replay often:
Jadie playing on the keys
as the house erupted in singing
"Down by the Riverside."

And in the subsequent days
after Mom flew away,
we sat around that table
on Grand Magnolia Dr.

We would sit into the night,
warming up plates made
from meals prepared and delivered
to us by all our other mothers.

So many that we had to keep
more than a handful frozen.
We would flow in and out of
laughter and silence.

Bouncing between questions
and the hesitancy of thinking
about what had taken place.

And yet there in that space
nothing made more sense.
Something of heaven opened up
and then left us as quickly
as it had come.

Paranormal Activity

Luke 24:36-38

Now I know what a ghost is.
Unfinished business, that's what.
SALMAN RUSHDIE,
THE SATANIC VERSES

And this ghost showed up
to tell us
The work is far from over.
We have only just begun.
Ghosts haunt us—
departing and returning
again and again.
Sweat drenching
the palms of our hands
each time.
The real fear we feel
is of keeping their work alive—
the fear that their dreams have died
with them,
and that we are inadequate
to breathe new life
into those dreams again.

FISH FRY

Luke 24:39-43

Fried fish had always been a fixture in our gatherings.
This unsung hero of family meals took on
new purpose in keeping our bonds strong.
Nafeesah Allen, "Fried Fish Is a Fixture
in Black American Cuisine"

Ain't nothing more down to earth,
touching the dirt,
than a fish fry.
Only the real ones know.

I'm talking about aunts with battered hands,
covered with buttermilk,
flour, and cornmeal.

Touch those hands
and feel the evidence of love.

There will be no doubt
of how real the love is
once that fish touches your lips.

Throw on some hot sauce
and you'll insist
that this is a Divine visitation.

Ascension

Luke 24:44-53

We are the revolutionary poem, exclamation point
You don't have to go home, but this is only the start
The good part is what comes next.

Morgan Parker, "Exclamation Point"

And this is what poetry does:
It carries us.

It invites us into a story,
    unfinished, saying:

        write the next stanza.

It gives us no plan,
        no blueprint for the future
        but simply asks us to witness—
        take it in and declare
        what we have seen.

It flies away but does not leave.
        Its presence remains
        long after the page
        has been turned—
        long after the last word
                spoken.

It leaves us with questions
        gazing toward heaven
for answers
        but no answer descends.

Its intent:
        to get us to sit
        with the questions again.

ACKNOWLEDGMENTS

My deepest appreciation and gratitude go to God: my Source and my muse. All of this is from you, for you, and to you.

Thank you to the family, friends, mentors, teachers, ancestors, poems, and lyrics that these poems were written with and written for. These poems were not written alone, but in the company of community. I am forever grateful.

Thank you to my wife and life partner, Genay. You read early drafts of these poems. You gave me time and space to write. You encouraged me to get started and to keep going. Neither of these first two collections exists without you. I love you with all my heart.

Thank you to my daughters, Zora and Suhaila. You both inspire me every day and fuel my imagination. These poems are filled with your magic.

Thank you to my father, Drew. *Touch the Earth* is for you.

Thank you to my mother, Debbie. You're always with us. Your presence is in each of these poems. I'm sure of it. We miss you.

Thank you to my brothers, Devon, Ki, Aaron, and Sean. You all have given me a lifetime of material for these poems.

Thank you to my editor, Ethan McCarthy, for trusting this project and for your painstaking work.

Thank you to my friend Pádraig Ó Tuama, not only for your beautiful foreword, but also for being one of my first readers and so tenderly caring for each poem.

Thank you to everyone who will take the time to sit with this book. These poems are not complete until they meet you, the reader.

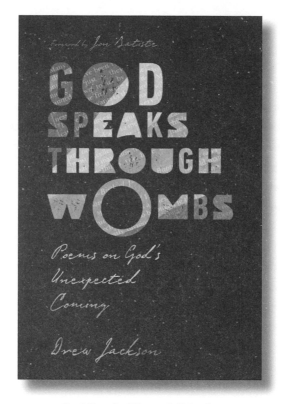

God Speaks Through Wombs
978-1-5140-0267-4